HISTORY'S MOST INFLUENTIAL MUSICIANS

FROM 1960 TO 2000

Aretha Franklin to Jay-Z

EDITED BY GINI GORLINSKI

Britannica Educational Publishing
IN ASSOCIATION WITH
ROSEN
EDUCATIONAL SERVICES

Published in 2024 by Britannica Educational Publishing
(a trademark of Encyclopædia Britannica, Inc.)
in association with Rosen Educational Services, LLC
2544 Clinton Street, Buffalo, NY 14224.

Distributed exclusively by Rosen Educational Services.
For a listing of additional Britannica Educational Publishing titles, call toll free (800) 237-9932.

First Edition

Britannica Educational Publishing
Michael I. Levy: Executive Editor
Marilyn L. Barton: Senior Coordinator, Production Control
Steven Bosco: Director, Editorial Technologies
Lisa S. Braucher: Senior Producer and Data Editor
Yvette Charboneau: Senior Copy Editor
Kathy Nakamura: Manager, Media Acquisition
Gini Gorlinski, Associate Editor, Music and Dance
Diana Solomon, Copy Editor

Editor: Greg Roza
Book design: Michael Flynn

Photo credits: Cover https://commons.wikimedia.org/wiki/File:Madonna1037_(21916900629)_(cropped).jpg; p. 9 https://commons.wikimedia.org/wiki/File:Popartiest_Jimi_Hendrix_op_Hippy_Happy_beurs_voor_jongeren_in_Ahoy.jpg; p. 15 https://commons.wikimedia.org/wiki/File:Ledzeppelin_posterpelo_1972.jpg; p. 24 https://commons.wikimedia.org/wiki/File:Bob_Marley_%26_The_Wailing_Wailers_Z%C3%BCrich_Com_L29-0351-0006-0003.tif#mw-jump-to-license; p. 31 https://en.wikipedia.org/wiki/File:David_Bowie_Ron_Frazier_1977.jpg; p. 36 https://commons.wikimedia.org/wiki/File:Bruce_Springsteen_20080815.jpg; p. 45 https://commons.wikimedia.org/wiki/File:Prince_Brussels_1986_(retouched).jpg; p. 51 https://commons.wikimedia.org/wiki/File:Michael_Jackson_Dangerous_World_Tour_1993.jpg; p. 56 Wikimedia.

Cataloging-in-Publication Data
Names: Gorlinski, Gini.
Title: Influential musicians: from 1960 to 2000—Aretha Franklin to Jay-Z / Gini Gorlinski.
Description: New York : Britannica Educational Publishing, in Association with Rosen Educational Services. 2024. | Series: History's most influential musicians | Includes glossary and index.
Identifiers: ISBN 9781499475067 (library bound) | ISBN 9781499475050 (pbk) | ISBN 9781499475074 (ebook)
Subjects: LCSH: Musicians--Biography--Juvenile literature. | Musicians--Juvenile literature.
Classification: LCC ML3929.G67 2024 | DDC 780.92'2 B--dc23

Manufactured in the United States of America

CPSIA Compliance Information: Batch #CSBRIT24. For further information contact Rosen Publishing at 1-800-237-9932.

CONTENTS

Introduction

"Music itself is going to become like running water or electricity."
—David Bowie

What is influence? Is it the power that one individual holds to change the world? Is it prestige—the glimmering reputation earned by those who have achieved excellence or superiority? Or is it that sense of immortality bestowed on certain people who, through their lives, their actions, and their accomplishments, have climbed pedestals so high and prominent that they are virtually guaranteed a place in the books of history?

Influence can mean so many things and is therefore hard to define. But this much is clear: in a book such as this, where the subject is influential musicians, an exact definition hardly matters. Such artists may exert themselves in all kinds of ways—through their compositions, lyrics, performances, or even through "extracurricular" activities such as raising funds for charitable causes and organizations.

Just by taking the stage—whether in a local church or on the 50-yard line during halftime at the Super Bowl—musicians have instant influence. They command the ability to make people stop what they are doing—to have them clap, dance, and sing along.

Aretha. Her first name alone is instantly recognizable, conjuring the image and sound of this singular musician. The undeniably sensational Aretha Franklin, better known to many as the "Queen of Soul," was the first woman to be inducted into the Rock and Roll Hall of Fame (1987). An electrifying performer since she premiered as a teenager in the mid-1950s, Aretha Franklin has used her unprecedented vocal talent to stir deep emotions in audiences at venues as varied and far-reaching as Detroit churches, Fillmore West in San Francisco, and the 2009 presidential inauguration of Barack Obama in Washington, D.C. Millions have bought her albums; millions more have not only heard but felt the energy of her voice.

The great Irish rock band U2 all but defines what it means to be influential. Bono, the band's lead singer, is also cofounder of the grassroots advocacy organization ONE and a regular contributor to newspapers. Through ONE, Bono has brought together millions of people committed to fighting extreme poverty and disease, especially in Africa. But it is the band's rock music, which Bono and a tight-knit group of friends (including David "the Edge" Evans; Larry Mullen, Jr.; and Adam Clayton) started in 1977, that has the most influence. Beginning with their first breakthrough album, War, U2 has over the years created music that is so instantly recognizable as theirs, yet also so innovative and so technologically cutting-edge, that you are practically compelled to listen. Influential? Certainly. How so? That is hard to say. In that they have reduced hunger? In that they have inspired teenagers to pick up an instrument? Or in the music that has followed their lead, from one new band to the next, and which clearly demonstrates a reverence for this celebrity group of post-punk rock stars.

Those musicians featured in this book span hundreds of years, countless musical genres, and immeasurable distances in style, technique, and purpose. Nevertheless, they have all been, and continue to be, influential. Some are influential because they brought a unique approach to their art that others later followed. Others were leaders of an influential movement in their field—a movement that led future musicians to improvise, change, and ultimately re-create music itself.

And still others, through their work, brought about social reform and societal change that has forever shaped the landscape in which we now live.

ARETHA FRANKLIN

(b. March 25, 1942, Memphis, Tenn., U.S.—d. Aug. 16, 2018, Detroit, Mich.)

American singer Aretha Louise Franklin defined the golden age of soul music of the 1960s.

Franklin's mother, Barbara, was a gospel singer and pianist. Her father, C.L. Franklin, presided over the New Bethel Baptist Church of Detroit, Michigan, and was a minister of national influence. A singer himself, he was noted for his brilliant sermons, many of which were recorded by Chess Records.

Franklin's parents separated when she was six, and she remained with her father in Detroit. Her mother died when Aretha was 10. As a young teen, Franklin performed with her father on his gospel programs in major cities throughout the country and was recognized as a vocal prodigy. Her central influence, Clara Ward of the renowned Ward Singers, was a family friend. Other gospel greats of the day—Albertina Walker and Jackie Verdell—helped shape young Franklin's style. Her album *The Gospel Sound of Aretha Franklin* (1956) captures the electricity of her performances as a 14-year-old.

At age 18, with her father's blessing, Franklin switched from sacred to secular music. She moved to New York City, where Columbia Records executive John Hammond, who had signed Count Basie and Billie Holiday, arranged her recording contract and supervised sessions highlighting her in a blues-jazz vein. From that first session, "Today I Sing the Blues" (1960) remains a classic. But, as her Detroit friends on the Motown label enjoyed hit after hit, Franklin struggled to achieve crossover success. Columbia placed her with a variety of producers who marketed her to both adults ("If Ever You Should Leave Me," 1963) and teens ("Soulville," 1964). Without targeting any particular genre, she sang everything from Broadway ballads to youth-oriented rhythm and blues. Critics recognized her talent, but the public remained lukewarm until 1966, when she switched to Atlantic Records, where producer Jerry Wexler allowed her to sculpt her own musical identity.

At Atlantic, Franklin returned to her gospel-blues roots, and the results were sensational. "I Never Loved a Man (the Way I Love You)" (1967), recorded at Fame Studios in Florence, Alabama, was her first million-seller. Surrounded by sympathetic musicians playing spontaneous arrangements and devising the background vocals herself, Franklin refined a style associated with Ray Charles—a rousing mixture of gospel and rhythm and blues—and raised it to new heights. As a civil rights-minded nation lent greater support to Black urban music, Franklin was crowned the "Queen of Soul." "Respect," her 1967 cover of Otis Redding's spirited composition, became an anthem operating on personal, sexual, and racial levels. "Think" (1968), which Franklin wrote herself, also had more than one meaning. For the next half-dozen years, she became a hit maker of unprecedented proportions; she was "Lady Soul."

In the early 1970s she triumphed at the Fillmore West in San Francisco before an audience of flower children and on whirlwind tours of Europe and Latin America. Her return to church, *Amazing Grace* (1972), is considered one of the great gospel albums of any era. By the late 1970s disco cramped Franklin's style and eroded her popularity. But in 1982, with help from singer-songwriter-producer Luther Vandross, she was back on top with a new label, Arista, and a new dance hit, "Jump to It," followed by "Freeway of Love" (1985). A reluctant interviewee, Franklin kept her private life private, claiming that the popular perception associating her with the unhappiness of singers

Bessie Smith and Billie Holiday was misinformed.

In 1987 Franklin became the first woman inducted into the Rock and Roll Hall of Fame. While her album sales in the 1990s and 2000s failed to approach the numbers of previous decades, Franklin remained the Queen of Soul, and in 2009 she electrified a crowd of more than one million with her performance of "My Country 'Tis of Thee" at the presidential inauguration of Barack Obama.

JIMI HENDRIX

(b. Nov. 27, 1942, Seattle, Wash., U.S.—d. Sept. 18, 1970, London, Eng.)

American rock guitarist, singer, and composer Jimi Hendrix fused American traditions of blues, jazz, rock, and soul with techniques of British avant-garde rock to redefine the electric guitar in his own image.

Though his active career as a featured artist lasted a mere four years, Hendrix altered the course of popular music and became one of the most successful and influential musicians of his era. An instrumentalist who radically redefined the expressive potential and sonic palette of the electric guitar, he was the composer of a classic repertoire of songs ranging from ferocious rockers to delicate, complex ballads. He also was the most charismatic in-concert performer of his generation. Moreover, he was a visionary who collapsed the genre boundaries of rock, soul, blues, and jazz and an iconic figure whose appeal linked the concerns of white hippies and Black revolutionaries by clothing Black anger in the colourful costumes of London's Carnaby Street.

A former paratrooper whose honourable medical discharge exempted him from service in the Vietnam War, Hendrix spent the early 1960s working as a freelance accompanist for a variety of musicians, both famous and

Jimi Hendrix performs at the Happy Hippy Fair in the Netherlands in 1967.

obscure. His unorthodox style and penchant for playing at high volume, however, limited him to subsistence-level work until he was discovered in a small New York City club and brought to England in August 1966. Performing alongside two British musicians, he stunned London's clubland with his instrumental virtuosity and extroverted showmanship. Members of the Beatles, the Rolling Stones, and the Who were among his admirers, but it proved a lot easier for Hendrix to learn their tricks than it was for them to learn his.

Hendrix had an encyclopaedic knowledge of the musical roots on which the cutting-edge rock of his time was based, but, thanks to his years on the road with the likes of Little Richard and the Isley Brothers, he also had hands-on experience of the cultural and social worlds in which those roots had developed and a great admiration for the work of Bob Dylan, the Beatles, and the Yardbirds. Speedily adapting the current musical and sartorial fashions of late 1966 London to his own needs, he was soon able not only to match the likes of the Who at their own high-volume, guitar-smashing game but also to top them with what rapidly became the hottest-ticket show in town.

By November his band, the Jimi Hendrix Experience, had their first Top Ten single, "Hey Joe." Two more hits, "Purple Haze" and "The Wind Cries Mary," followed before their first album, *Are You Experienced?*, was released in the summer of 1967, when it was second in impact only to the Beatles' *Sgt. Pepper's Lonely Hearts Club Band*. Its immediate successor, *Axis: Bold as Love*, followed that December. Hendrix was flown to California for a scene-stealing appearance at the Monterey Pop Festival, which rendered him a sensation in his homeland less than a year after his departure.

Relocating back to the United States in 1968, he enjoyed further acclaim with the sprawling, panoramic double album *Electric Ladyland*, but the second half of his career proved frustrating. Legal complications from an old contract predating his British sojourn froze his recording royalties, necessitating constant touring to pay his bills; and his audiences were reluctant to allow him to progress beyond the musical blueprint of his earliest successes. He was on the verge of solving both these problems when he died of an overdose of barbiturates. In his all-too brief career, Hendrix managed to combine and extend the soaring improvisational transcendence of John Coltrane, the rhythmic virtuosity of James Brown, the bluesy intimacy of John Lee Hooker, the lyrical aesthetic of Bob Dylan, the bare-knuckle onstage aggression of the Who, and the hallucinatory studio fantasias of the Beatles. His work provides a continuing source of inspiration to successive generations of musicians to whom he remains a touchstone for emotional honesty, technological innovation, and an all-inclusive vision of cultural and social brotherhood.

JONI MITCHELL

(b. Nov. 7, 1943, Fort McLeod, Alta., Can.)

Canadian experimental singer-songwriter Joni Mitchell (born Roberta Joan Anderson) enjoyed her greatest popularity in the 1970s. Like her contemporary of the 1960s, Bob Dylan, she helped turn pop music into an art form.

Mitchell studied commercial art in her native Alberta before moving to Toronto in 1964 and performing at local folk clubs and coffeehouses. After a brief marriage to folksinger Chuck Mitchell, she relocated to New York City, where in 1967 she made her eponymous debut album (also known as *Songs to a Seagull*). This concept album was acclaimed for the maturity of its lyrics.

With each successive release, Mitchell gained a larger following, from *Clouds* (which in 1969 won a Grammy Award for best folk performance) to the mischievous euphoria of *Ladies of the Canyon* (1970) to *Blue* (1971), which was her first million-selling album. By the early 1970s Mitchell had branched out from her acoustic base to experiment with rock and jazz, with *The Hissing of Summer Lawns* (1975) marking her transition to a more complex, layered sound. Whereas earlier albums were more confessional in their subject matter, *The Hissing of Summer Lawns*, on which she satirized the role of the 1970s housewife, showed Mitchell's movement toward social observation. Although she had a number of pop hits, especially in 1970 with "Big Yellow Taxi" and "Woodstock," Mitchell's impact was as a long-term "album artist." With its carefully precise yet improvisational feel, her music is at times difficult to listen to. She does not opt for straight melody or satisfying conclusions. "My music is not designed to grab instantly. It's designed to wear for a lifetime, to hold up like a fine cloth," she once said.

With *Hejira* (1976) and *Don Juan's Reckless Daughter* (1977), she continued to disregard commercial considerations, while *Mingus* (1979) was considered by many as beyond the pale. An album that began as a collaboration with the jazz bassist Charles Mingus ended up as a treatment of his themes after his death. Mitchell delved not only deeper into jazz but also into Black history; the album was as much a voice for the dispossessed as it was a biography of Mingus.

Having proved that she could make commercially successful albums and win critical acclaim, Mitchell became a prestige artist. Moreover, because her songs had become hits for others, she was a source of considerable publishing revenue for her record companies. As a result, they went along with her musical experiments. After *Mingus*, however, Mitchell stood back a little from the pop world. From the beginning of her career she had illustrated her own album covers, so it was not surprising that in the 1980s she began to develop her visual art, undecided about whether to concentrate more on painting or music.

Although not as prolific as in the 1960s and '70s, Mitchell continued to create penetrating, imaginative music, from *Dog Eat Dog* (1985) to the more reflective *Night Ride Home* (1991) and the Grammy Award-winning *Turbulent Indigo* (1994). Having dealt with international political and social issues such as Ethiopian famine on *Dog Eat Dog*, she returned, by the early 1990s, to more personal subject matter—singing about true love, for instance, on *Turbulent Indigo*. One of the first women in modern rock to achieve enviable longevity and critical recognition, Mitchell has been a major inspiration to everyone from Dylan and Prince to a later generation of female artists such as Suzanne Vega and Alanis Morissette. Although she regularly collaborated with producers and arrangers,—Mitchell always had control over her material. Her songs have been covered by a range of stars, including Dylan, Fairport Convention, Judy Collins, Johnny Cash, and Crosby, Stills and Nash. Though unworried about pop chart trends, in 1997 she enjoyed major success with a new, young audience when Janet Jackson sampled from Mitchell's *Big Yellow Taxi* for the massive hit *Got 'Til It's Gone*. In 1997 she published a new collection of her work, entitled *Joni Mitchell: The Complete Poems and Lyrics*. That year she was also inducted into the Rock and Roll Hall of Fame.

LED ZEPPELIN

The members were Jimmy Page (b. Jan. 9, 1944, Heston, Middlesex, Eng.), Robert Plant (b. Aug. 20, 1948, West Bromwich, West Midlands, Eng.), John Paul Jones (original name John Baldwin; b. Jan. 3, 1946, Sidcup, Kent, Eng.), and John Bonham (b. May 31, 1948, Redditch, Hereford and Worcester, Eng.—d. Sept. 25, 1980, Windsor, Berkshire).

The British rock band Led Zeppelin was extremely popular in the 1970s, and although their musical style was diverse, they came to be well known for their influence on the development of heavy metal.

Initially called the New Yardbirds, Led Zeppelin was formed in 1968 by Jimmy Page, the final lead guitarist for the legendary British blues band the Yardbirds. Bassist and keyboard player Jones, like Page, was a veteran studio musician; vocalist Plant and drummer Bonham came from little-known provincial bands. The group was influenced by various kinds of music, including early rock and roll, psychedelic rock, blues, folk, Celtic, Indian, and Arabic music. Although acoustic and folk-based music was part of the band's repertoire from its inception, it was the bottom-heavy, loud, raw, and powerful electric style that gained them their following and notoriety early on; their first two albums included many of the songs that prompted Led Zeppelin's categorization as a precursor of heavy metal. The heaviness of songs such as "Dazed and Confused" and "Whole Lotta Love" was created by Bonham's enormous drum sound and through Page's production techniques, in which he emphasized drums and bass, resulting in a sonic spaciousness that has kept the records sounding fresh years after they were made. Page and Jones also wrote most of the band's music, while Plant contributed lyrics and some musical ideas. Although Page was responsible for the majority of their signature riffs (the short, repeated

Led Zeppelin, pictured in 1972, initially formed as the New Yardbirds.

musical ideas that often structure a song), Jones wrote the riff for the celebrated "Black Dog" and several other songs. Jones also contributed much to the arrangement of songs. Page's guitar solos were based primarily on melodic ideas derived from the blues scale ("Heartbreaker" is a good example), and he is especially known for creating multiple, simultaneous guitar parts—a kind of guitar orchestra—in such songs as "Achilles Last Stand" and "The Song Remains the Same." Page is considered one of rock's guitar heroes, but, because he was more interested in creating a distinctive mood and sound on a recording than in displaying his virtuosity, he frequently chose not to include a guitar solo in Zeppelin songs.

Plant's voice rounded out Led Zeppelin's sound. Exaggerating the vocal style and expressive palette of blues singers such as Howlin' Wolf and Muddy Waters, Plant created the sound that has defined much hard rock and heavy metal singing: a high range, an abundance of distortion, loud volume, and emotional excess ("Whole Lotta Love" is a classic example). Plant was, however, capable of a broader stylistic range, including tender ballads ("The Rain Song") and songs showing the influence of Indian and Arabic vocal styles ("Kashmir").

Led Zeppelin's best-known song is "Stairway to Heaven"; its gentle acoustic beginning eventually builds to an exhilarating climax featuring a lengthy electric guitar solo. This combination of acoustic and electric sections was typical for Page, who from the band's beginning was interested in juxtaposing what he called "light and shade." The song appeared on the band's fourth and most famous album, released untitled, which showed only four runic symbols (intended to represent the band members) on the cover and had the mystical, mythological lyrics to "Stairway" printed on the inner sleeve. The sense of mystery and ritual that this created became an important part of the band's image.

Thanks in part to their manager, Peter Grant, the band enjoyed phenomenal commercial success throughout the 1970s. While Led Zeppelin never received the kind of critical acclaim or mainstream acceptance accorded the Beatles or the Rolling Stones, their influence on rock music has been prodigious. They are regularly cited as the progenitors of both hard rock and heavy metal. Their sound has been imitated by bands from Black Sabbath to Nirvana. They also inspired hard rock bands to include acoustic elements in their music and were among the first to experiment with Indian and North African music. Page's style has served as an important model for most rock guitarists, and Bonham is often cited as the model for metal or hard rock drumming.

Led Zeppelin disbanded in 1980 after Bonham's accidental death. The group re-formed for short, one-off performances in 1985 (the Live Aid benefit), 1988 (Atlantic Records' 40th anniversary concert), and 1995 (the band's induction into the Rock and Roll Hall of Fame). Much more momentous was the group's full-blown concert in London in December 2007 to honour Atlantic's legendary cofounder Ahmet Ertegun, at which Bonham's son, Jason, played the drums.

THE WHO

The principal members were Pete Townshend (b. May 19, 1945, London, Eng.), Roger Daltrey (b. March 1, 1944, London, Eng.), John Entwistle (b. Oct. 9, 1944, London, Eng.—d. June 27, 2002, Las Vegas, Nev., U.S.), and Keith Moon (b. Aug. 23, 1946, London. Eng.—d. Sept. 7, 1978, London). Moon was replaced by Kenny Jones (b. Sept. 16, 1948, London, Eng.).

The Who was a British rock group that was among the most popular and influential bands of the 1960s and '70s and that originated the rock opera.

Though primarily inspired by American rhythm and blues, the Who took a bold step toward defining a uniquely British rock vernacular in the 1960s. Eschewing the Beatles' idealized romance and the Rolling Stones' cocky swagger, the Who shunned pretension and straightforwardly dealt with teenage travails. At a time when rock music was uniting young people all over the world, the Who were friendless, bitter outsiders.

Townshend and Entwistle joined Daltrey in his group, the Detours, in 1962; with drummer Doug Sandom they became, in turn, the Who and the High Numbers. Moon replaced Sandom in early 1964, after which the group released a self-consciously mod single ("I'm the Face") to little notice and became the Who again in late 1964. The West London quartet cultivated a Pop art image to suit the fashion-obsessed British "mod" subculture and matched that look with the rhythm-and-blues sound that mod youth favoured. Townshend ultimately acknowledged that clothing made from the Union Jack, sharp suits, pointy boots, and short haircuts were a contrivance, but it did the trick, locking in a fanatically devoted core following. Fashion, however, was strictly a starting point for the Who; by the late 1960s the mods were history, and the Who were long past needing to identify themselves with the uniform of any movement.

The band's early records dealt with alienation, uncertainty, and frustration, lashing out with tough lyrics, savage power chords and squalling feedback by guitarist-songwriter Townshend, the kinetic assault of drummer Moon and bassist Entwistle, and the macho brawn of singer Daltrey. The four singles that introduced the Who between January 1965 and March 1966—"I Can't Explain,"

"Anyway, Anyhow, Anywhere," "My Generation," and "Substitute"—declared themselves in an unprecedented fury of compressed sonic aggression, an artistic statement intensified onstage by Townshend's habit of smashing his guitar to climax concerts. While other groups were moving toward peace-and-love idealism, the Who sang of unrequited lust ("Pictures of Lily"), peer pressure ("Happy Jack"), creepy insects (Entwistle's "Boris the Spider"), and gender confusion ("I'm a Boy"). As one instrument after another ended in splinters, the Who firmly declared themselves proponents of making violent rage a form of rock catharsis.

Until the 1967 release of *The Who Sell Out*, a sardonic concept album presented as a pirate radio broadcast, the Who were primarily a singles group. They were, however, more successful in this regard in Britain than in the United States ("I Can See for Miles," released in 1967, was the group's only *Billboard* Top Ten single). It was the 1969 rock opera *Tommy*—and a memorable performance at Woodstock that summer—that made the Who a world-class album-rock act. In the process, Townshend was recognized as one of rock's most intelligent, articulate, and self-conscious composers.

The Who cemented their standing with *Who's Next* (1971), an album of would-be teen anthems ("Won't Get Fooled Again," "Baba O'Riley") and sensitive romances ("Behind Blue Eyes," "Love Ain't for Keeping"), all reflecting Townshend's dedication to his "avatar," the Indian mystic Meher Baba. That same year, Entwistle released a solo album, the darkly amusing *Smash Your Head Against the Wall*; Townshend issued his first solo album, *Who Came First*, in 1972; and Daltrey offered his, *Daltrey*, in 1973. Still, the Who continued apace, releasing Townshend's second magnum rock opera, *Quadrophenia*, in 1973, *The Who by Numbers* in 1975, and *Who Are You* in 1978.

Moon ("the Loon"), whose excessive lifestyle was legendary, died of an accidental drug overdose in 1978 and was replaced by Jones. So constituted, the Who released *Face Dances* (1981) and *It's Hard* (1982) before disbanding in 1982. Daltrey pursued acting while letting his solo career taper off. Entwistle released occasional records to little effect. Townshend busied himself briefly as a book editor while undertaking a variety of solo ventures—from well-received Who-like rock records such as *Empty Glass* (1980) to *The Iron Man* (1989), a less-successful experiment in musical theatre that nevertheless paved the way for the triumphant delivery of *Tommy* to Broadway in 1993. Townshend, Daltrey, and Entwistle reunited for tours in 1989 and 1996–97. The Who was about to embark on a U.S. tour in 2002 when Entwistle died.

Tommy remains the Who's most enduring creation. On its way to the theatre, *Tommy* became an all-star orchestral album in 1972 and a garish film with Daltrey in the title role in 1975. *Quadrophenia* also was made into a film, in 1979, and was revived by the touring Who as a stagy rock spectacle in the 1990s.

In 2005 and 2006 Townshend serialized a novella, *The Boy Who Heard Music*, online, and a set of related songs constituted *Wire & Glass*, the mini-opera that made up part of *Endless Wire* (2006), which was the first album of new Who material since 1982. A full-blown musical based on this material and also titled *The Boy Who Heard Music* premiered in July 2007 at Vassar College in Poughkeepsie, N.Y. A year later the Who were celebrated (and performed) at a VH1 Rock Honors concert.

BOB MARLEY

(b. Feb. 6, 1945, Nine Miles, St. Ann, Jam.—d. May 11, 1981, Miami, Fla., U.S.)

The thoughtful, ongoing distillation of early ska, rock steady, and reggae forms by Jamaican singer-songwriter Bob Marley blossomed in the 1970s into an electrifying rock-influenced hybrid that made the musician an international superstar.

The son of a white rural overseer, Norval Sinclair Marley, and the Black daughter of a local *custos* (respected backwoods squire), the former Cedella Malcolm, Bob Marley would forever remain the unique product of parallel worlds—his poetic worldview was shaped by the countryside, his music by the tough West Kingston ghetto streets. Marley's maternal grandfather was not just a prosperous farmer but also a bush doctor adept at the mysticism-steeped herbal healing that guaranteed respect in Jamaica's remote hill country. As a child Marley was known for his shy aloofness, his startling stare, and his penchant for palm reading. Virtually kidnapped by his absentee father (who had been disinherited by his own prominent family for marrying a Black woman), the preadolescent Marley was taken to live with an elderly woman in Kingston until a family friend rediscovered the boy by chance and returned him to Nine Miles.

By his early teens Marley was back in West Kingston, living in a government-subsidized tenement in Trench Town, a desperately poor slum. In the early 1960s, while a schoolboy serving an apprenticeship as a welder, Marley was exposed to the languid, jazz-infected shuffle-beat rhythms of ska, a Jamaican amalgam of American rhythm and blues and native mento (folk-calypso) strains then catching on commercially. Marley was a fan of Fats

Domino, the Moonglows, and pop singer Ricky Nelson, but, when his big chance came in 1961 to record with producer Leslie Kong, he cut "Judge Not," a peppy ballad he had written based on rural maxims learned from his grandfather. Among his other early tracks was "One Cup of Coffee," issued in 1963 in England on the Island Records label.

Marley also formed a vocal group in Trench Town with friends who would later be known as Peter Tosh (original name Winston Hubert MacIntosh) and Bunny Wailer (original name Neville O'Reilly Livingston). The trio, which named itself the Wailers (because, as Marley stated, "We started out crying"), received vocal coaching by noted singer Joe Higgs. Later they were joined by vocalist Junior Braithwaite and backup singers Beverly Kelso and Cherry Green.

In December 1963 the Wailers entered Coxsone Dodd's Studio One facilities to cut "Simmer Down," a song by Marley that he had used to win a talent contest in Kingston. "Simmer Down" was an urgent anthem from the shantytown precincts of the Kingston underclass. A huge overnight smash, it played an important role in recasting the agenda for stardom in Jamaican music circles. No longer did one have to parrot the stylings of overseas entertainers; it was possible to write raw, uncompromising songs for and about the disenfranchised people of the West Indian slums.

This bold stance transformed both Marley and his island nation, engendering the urban poor with a pride that would become a pronounced source of identity in Jamaican culture—as would the Wailers' Rastafarian faith, a creed popular among the impoverished people of the Caribbean, who worshiped the late Ethiopian emperor Haile Selassie I as the African redeemer foretold in popular quasi-biblical prophecy. The Wailers did well in Jamaica during the mid-1960s with their ska records, even during Marley's sojourn to Delaware in 1966 to visit his relocated mother and find temporary work. Reggae material created in 1969–71 increased the contemporary stature of the Wailers; and, once they signed in 1972 with the (by that time) international label Island and released *Catch a Fire*, their uniquely rock-contoured reggae gained a global audience. It also earned the charismatic Marley superstar status, which gradually led to the dissolution of the original triumvirate about early 1974. Although Peter Tosh would enjoy a distinguished solo career before his murder in 1987, many of his best solo albums (such as *Equal Rights* [1977]) were underappreciated, as was Bunny Wailer's excellent solo album *Blackheart Man* (1976).

Eric Clapton's version of the Wailers' "I Shot the Sheriff" in 1974 spread Marley's fame. Meanwhile, Marley continued to guide the skilled Wailers band through a series of potent, topical albums. By this point Marley also was backed by a trio of female vocalists that included his wife, Rita; she, like many of Marley's children, later experienced her own recording success. Featuring eloquent songs like "No Woman No Cry," "Exodus," "Could You Be Loved," "Coming in from the Cold," "Jamming," and "Redemption Song," Marley's landmark albums included *Natty Dread* (1974), *Live!* (1975), *Rastaman Vibration* (1976), *Exodus* (1977), *Kaya* (1978), *Uprising* (1980), and the posthumous *Confrontation* (1983). Exploding in Marley's reedy tenor, his songs were public expressions of personal truths—eloquent in their uncommon mesh of rhythm and blues, rock, and venturesome reggae forms and electrifying in their narrative might.

He also loomed large as a political figure and in 1976 survived what was believed to have been a politically

Jamaican singer-songwriter Bob Marley performing live on stage.

motivated assassination attempt. Marley's attempt to broker a truce between Jamaica's warring political factions led in April 1978 to his headlining the "One Love" peace concert. His sociopolitical clout also earned him an invitation to perform in 1980 at the ceremonies celebrating majority rule and internationally recognized independence for Zimbabwe. In April 1981, the Jamaican government awarded Marley the Order of Merit. A month later he died of cancer.

Although his songs were some of the best-liked and most critically acclaimed music in the popular canon, Marley was far more renowned in death than he had been in life. *Legend* (1984), a retrospective of his work, became the best-selling reggae album ever, with international sales of more than 12 million copies.

ERIC CLAPTON

(b. March 30, 1945, Ripley, Surrey, Eng.)

British rock musician Eric Clapton (born Eric Patrick Clapp) was a highly influential guitarist in the late 1960s and early 1970s and later became a major singer-songwriter.

Clapton was raised by his grandparents after his mother abandoned him at an early age. He began playing the guitar in his teens and briefly studied at the Kingston College of Art. After playing lead guitar with two minor bands, in 1963 he joined the Yardbirds, a rhythm-and-blues group in which his blues-influenced playing and commanding technique began to attract attention. Clapton left the Yardbirds in 1965 when they pursued commercial success with a pop-oriented style. That same year he joined John Mayall's Bluesbreakers, and his guitar playing soon became the group's principal drawing card as it attracted a fanatic following on the London club scene.

In 1966 Clapton left the Bluesbreakers to form a new band with two other virtuoso rock musicians, bassist Jack Bruce and drummer Ginger Baker. This group, Cream, achieved international popularity with its sophisticated, high-volume fusion of rock and blues that featured improvisatory solos. Clapton's mastery of blues form and phrasing, his rapid runs, and his plaintive vibrato were widely imitated by other rock guitarists. The high energy and emotional intensity of his playing on such songs as "Crossroads" and "White Room" set the standard for the rock guitar solo. Cream disbanded in late 1968, however, after having recorded such albums as *Disraeli Gears* (1967), *Wheels of Fire* (1968), and *Goodbye* (1969).

In 1969 Clapton and Baker formed the group Blind Faith with keyboardist-vocalist Steve Winwood and bassist Rick Grech, but the group broke up after recording only one album. Clapton emerged as a capable vocalist on his first solo album, which was released in 1970. He soon assembled a trio of strong session musicians (bassist Carl Radle, drummer Jim Gordon, and keyboardist Bobby Whitlock) into a new band called Derek and the Dominos, with Clapton as lead guitarist, vocalist, and songwriter. The guitarist Duane Allman joined the group in making the classic double album *Layla and Other Assorted Love Songs* (1970), which is regarded as Clapton's masterpiece and a landmark among rock recordings. Disappointed by *Layla*'s lacklustre sales and addicted to heroin, Clapton went into seclusion for two years. Overcoming his addiction, he made a successful comeback with the album *461 Ocean Boulevard* (1974), which included his hit remake of Bob Marley's "I Shot the Sheriff." On the album Clapton adopted a more relaxed approach that emphasized his songwriting and vocal abilities rather than his guitar playing. Over the next 20 years Clapton produced a string of albums, including

Slowhand (1977), *Backless* (1978), *Money and Cigarettes* (1983), *August* (1986), *Unplugged* (1992)—which featured the Top Five hit "Tears in Heaven," written after the death of his son—and *From the Cradle* (1994). He explored his musical influences with a pair of Grammy-winning collaborations: *Riding with the King* (2000) with blues legend B.B. King and *The Road to Escondido* (2006) with roots guitarist J.J. Cale. The critical and commercial success of these albums solidified his stature as one of the world's greatest rock musicians. *Clapton*, an autobiography, was published in 2007. In 2000 Clapton was inducted into the Rock and Roll Hall of Fame.

KING SUNNY ADE

(b. Sept. 1, 1946, Oshogbo, Nigeria)

Nigerian popular musician Sunday Adeniyi, popularly known as King Sunny Ade, was in the vanguard of the development and international popularization of juju music—a fusion of traditional Yoruba vocal forms and percussion with Western rock and roll.

"King" Sunny Ade enjoyed noble status not only through birth into the Yoruba royalty of southwestern Nigeria but also through popular acclaim as the "King of Juju" since the late 1970s. In his youth Ade played highlife, a type of urban dance music that emerged in Ghana in the late 19th century and blended elements of church music, military brass-band music, sea shanties, and various local African traditions. In the mid-1960s Ade abandoned highlife for juju, a related musical genre that arose in Nigeria in the 1920s as an expression of the urban Yoruba working class. He assembled his own juju band, the Green Spots, which he later renamed the African Beats, reflecting the re-Africanization of the genre that had been occurring since the early 1950s in conjunction with a growing sense of nationalism.

Prior to Ade's formation of the African Beats, one of his most notable predecessors, I.K. Dairo, had already modified juju through incorporation of Yoruba "talking" drums—which replicate the tones of Yoruba language—and through extensive use of the call-and-response vocal structure that is typical of the traditional music of many sub-Saharan African peoples, including the Yoruba. Upon this musical foundation, Ade laid a tapestry of guitar voices infused with the rhythmic and melodic colors of rock and roll. Ade's early albums with the African Beats, most notably *Sound Vibration* (1977) and *The Royal Sound* (1979), were tremendously successful, and, when the press declared Ade the King of Juju in 1977, the title became integral to his professional persona.

In the early 1980s Ade signed with Island Records, and the release of *Juju Music* (1982) propelled him, his band, and juju into the international limelight. Ade's next album with Island, the synthesizer-enriched *Synchro System* (1983), drew an even more thunderous response and prompted a surge in international bookings. By the mid-1980s Ade had exposed much of the non-African world to Nigerian juju. After his separation from Island in 1985, Ade focused his musical activity at home, at which time he also began to shift the topics of his lyrics from the ills of Nigerian society to more-intimate matters of personal struggle. Although he maintained a tight schedule of recording and performances in Nigeria, he continued to make intermittent appearances abroad on the rapidly expanding world music concert and festival circuit, where both he and juju music continued to enjoy a strong following.

DAVID BOWIE

(b. Jan. 8, 1947, London, Eng.—d. Jan. 10, 2016, New York, N.Y.)

British singer, songwriter, and actor David Bowie (born David Robert Jones) was most prominent in the 1970s and best known for his distinctive voice, shifting personae, and prescient sense of musical trends.

To call Bowie a transitional figure in rock history is less a judgment than a job description. Every niche he ever found was on a cusp, and he was at home nowhere else—certainly not in the unmoneyed London suburb where his childhood was as reserved as his adult life would be glamorous.

Gifted as a musician, actor, writer, and artist (Bowie attended art school from the age of 12), he would ultimately find his place as a performer utilizing all these skills. Nothing if not an eclectic musician in his own right, Bowie had similarly diverse tastes regarding the work of others, being an admirer of the showmanship of British actor and musician Anthony Newley as well as the romantic lyricism of Belgian musician Jacques Brel.

During the mod era of the 1960s Bowie fronted various bands from whose shadow he—having renamed himself to avoid confusion with the singer of the Monkees—emerged as a solo singer-songwriter. "Space Oddity," the science-fiction single that marks the real beginning of his career, reached the Top Ten in Britain in 1969, the song's well-timed release coming just after the Apollo 11 Moon mission. Bowie's third album, *The Man Who Sold the World* (1970), displayed an unprecedented hybrid of folk, art rock, and heavy metal sounds. But it wasn't until *Hunky Dory* (1971) that Bowie became truly popular, the hit single "Changes" being the prime vector of that fame.

The singer's ever-changing appearance, too, created a record-selling buzz. At once lighthearted and portentous,

Bowie's dramatic chameleonlike approach was tailor-made for the 1970s, his signature decade. Bowie created a series of inspired, daringly grandiose pastiches that insisted on utopia by depicting its alternative as inferno, beginning with the emblematic rock-star martyr fantasy *The Rise and Fall of Ziggy Stardust and the Spiders from Mars* (1972). In the process he stayed so hard on the heels of the zeitgeist that the doom-saying of *Diamond Dogs* (1974) and the disco romanticism of *Young Americans* (1975) were released less than a year apart.

Bowie's public disclosure of his bisexuality, rather than derailing his growing popularity, boosted his enigmatic allure. Similarly, his later recantation of such sexual proclivities had no negative affect on his career. Yet all this public display of personal matters took a private toll. By 1977 Bowie had decamped, ditching his idiosyncratic version of the main-stream for the avant-garde austerities of the minimalist album *Low*, a collaboration in Berlin with Brian Eno, the influential musician and producer who is perhaps best known for his ambient albums. As music, *Low* and its sequels, *Heroes* (1977) and *Lodger* (1979), would prove to be Bowie's most influential and lasting, serving as a blueprint for a later generation of techno-rock. In the short run, the albums marked the end of his significant mass audience impact, though not his sales. In addition to Eno, Bowie also collaborated with guitarists Mick Ronson and Carlos Alomar as well as ace nouveau-funk producer Nile Rodgers for "Let's Dance" (1983).

In the 1980s, despite the impressive artistic resolve of *Scary Monsters* (1980) and the equally impressive commercial success of *Let's Dance* (1983), which produced three American Top 20 hits, Bowie's once-innovative work seemed to have lost the musical, intellectual, and boundary-pushing edge of his previous efforts. In tandem with an acting career that, since his arresting debut in Nicolas Roeg's *The Man Who Fell to Earth* (1976), largely failed to jell, his vague later

As an actor, David Bowie appeared in Labyrinth *and* The Prestige.

albums oscillated between would-be commercial moves for which he did not seem to have the heart (*Never Let Me Down* [1987]) and would-be artistic statements for which he had lost his shrewdness (*Outside* [1995]). Yet his 1970s work including, in addition to his own output, service as a producer on landmark albums from Mott the Hoople, Lou Reed, and Iggy and the Stooges remains a vital and compelling index to a time it did its part to shape. Bowie was inducted into the Rock and Roll Hall of Fame in 1996. Ten years later, he was awarded the Grammy Lifetime Achievement Award.

NUSRAT FATEH ALI KHAN

(b. Oct. 13, 1948, Lyallpur [now Faisalabad] Pak.—d. Aug. 16, 1997, London, Eng.)

Pakistani singer Nusrat Fateh Ali Khan is considered one of the greatest performers of *qawwali*, a Sufi Muslim devotional music characterized by simple melodies, forceful rhythms, and energetic improvisations that encourage a state of euphoria in the listener.

Nusrat's father, Ustad Fateh Ali Khan, and two of his uncles, Ustad Mubarik Ali Khan and Ustad Salamat Ali Khan, were famous *qawwal*s (practitioners of *qawwali*) who sang in the classical form. Although Nusrat began to display a penchant for music and a particular aptitude for singing before he had reached age 10, he did not begin to devote himself to the *qawwali* tradition until he sang at his father's funeral in 1964. Two years later he gave his first public performance as a *qawwal*, singing with his uncles, with whom he continued to perform until 1971, when Ustad Mubarik died.

Qawwali originated in 12th-century Persia. The lyrics are based on medieval Sufi poems that often use images of romantic love to express deep religious faith. The traditionally male *qawwal*, who knows these poems by heart, unites phrases and passages from different poems to create a new expression. *Qawwali* performances are typically held in shrines and are marked by passionate shouting and dancing. *Qawwali* is similar in spirit to American gospel music.

Following his father's death, Nusrat continued to study the recordings of his father and uncles, using them as a springboard from which to develop his own style. Within just a few years he had established himself throughout Pakistan as the outstanding *qawwal* of his generation, singing powerfully and expressively in a very high register (a family trademark), with remarkable stamina and melodic creativity. In concert he was usually accompanied by tabla (a pair of single-headed drums played with the hands), harmoniums (or reed organs; small keyboard instruments with a foot-operated bellows), and backing vocals.

As he matured as a performer, Nusrat made various adjustments to his style, such as increasing the tempo, as a means to elevate *qawwali* to a new level of aesthetic and spiritual resonance with contemporary—and international—audiences. In 1985 he gave a concert in the United Kingdom, and word of his talent began to spread. He was soon performing regularly throughout Europe. He first toured the United States in 1989, and in the 1990s he contributed to the sound tracks of several popular films. Nusrat also worked with a number of internationally recognized figures in popular and art music. Popular musician Peter Gabriel promoted Nusrat on the world music circuit through his WOMAD (World of Music, Arts and Dance) festivals and through recordings on his Real World Records label. Meanwhile, composer Michael Brook helped increase the accessibility of Nusrat's vocalizations by recasting them within Western rhythmic frameworks. Nusrat believed in the universality of the musical message and strove throughout his career to make his music transcend religious and cultural boundaries. When he died suddenly in 1997, Nusrat was mourned by fans across the globe.

BRUCE SPRINGSTEEN

(b. Sept. 23, 1949, Freehold, N.J., U.S.)

American singer, songwriter, and bandleader Bruce Springsteen became the archetypal rock performer of the 1970s and '80s.

Springsteen grew up in Freehold, a mill town where his father worked as a labourer. His rebellious and artistic side led him to the nearby Jersey shore, where his imagination was sparked by the rock band scene and the boardwalk life, high and low. After an apprenticeship in bar bands on the mid-Atlantic coast, Springsteen turned himself into a solo singer-songwriter in 1972 and auditioned for talent scout John Hammond, Sr., who immediately signed him to Columbia Records. His first two albums, released in 1973, reflect folk rock, soul, and rhythm-and-blues influences, especially those of Van Morrison, Bob Dylan, and Stax/Volt Records. Springsteen's voice, a rough baritone that he used to shout on up-tempo numbers and to more sensual effect on slower songs, was shown to good effect here, but his sometimes spectacular guitar playing, which ranged from dense power chord effects to straight 1950s rock and roll, had to be downplayed to fit the singer-songwriter format.

With his third album, *Born to Run* (1975), Springsteen transformed into a full-fledged rock and roller, heavily indebted to Phil Spector and Roy Orbison. The album, a diurnal song cycle, was a sensation even before it hit the shelves; indeed, the week of the album's release, Columbia's public relations campaign landed Springsteen on the covers of both *Time* and *Newsweek*. Three years passed before the follow-up, the darker, tougher *Darkness on the Edge of Town* (1978), appeared. With "Hungry Heart," from *The River* (1980), Springsteen finally scored an international hit single.

By then, however, he was best known for his stage shows, three- and four-hour extravaganzas with his E Street Band that blended rock, folk, and soul with dramatic intensity and exuberant humour. The band, a crew of mixed stereotypes—from rock-and-roll bandit to cool music professional—was more like a gang than a musical unit, apparently held together by little other than faith in its leader. Springsteen's refusal, after *Born to Run*, to cooperate with much of the record company's public relations and marketing machinery, coupled with his painstaking recording process and the draining live shows, helped earn his reputation as a performer of principle as well as of power and popularity.

Nebraska (1982), a stark set of acoustic songs, most in some way concerned with death, was an unusual interlude. It was *Born in the U.S.A.* (1984) and his subsequent 18-month world tour that cinched Springsteen's reputation as the preeminent writer-performer of his rock-and-roll period. Springsteen's social perspective has been distinctly working-class throughout his career, a point emphasized both by his 1995 album, *The Ghost of Tom Joad*, which concerned itself with the economically and spiritually destitute in America and by his 1994 hit single (his first in eight years), the AIDS-related "Streets of Philadelphia," from the film *Philadelphia*, for which he won both an Academy Award and a Grammy Award.

The other side of Springsteen's work is reflected in the albums that he produced in the period beginning with *Tunnel of Love* (1987) and including *Human Touch* and *Lucky Town* (released simultaneously in 1992). The songs on these

Bruce Springsteen and Max Weinberg on drums perform in 2008.

albums are intensely personal reflections on intimate relationships. In general, they have not been as popular.

Bridging all this is the five-record set *Bruce Springsteen and the E Street Band Live 1975–1985* (1986), which captures as much of his highly visual stage show of that period as can be rendered in a solely audio form. The breakup of the E Street Band in 1989 and general trends in pop music fashion curbed Springsteen's popularity. In 1998 he put together a box set, *Tracks*, consisting for the most part of leftover material that had failed to make the cut on his albums with the band. This grandiose gesture established him as prolix beyond all but a couple of peers. Sales of *Tracks* were trivial compared with those for *Live*.

In 1999 Springsteen reunited the E Street Band. They appeared with him when he alone was inducted into the Rock and Roll Hall of Fame in early 1999, then spent a year touring with him, resulting in a live album (*Live in New York City* [2001]) but only a handful of new songs. On Sept. 21, 2001, Springsteen performed the national debut of his song "My City of Ruins" on a television special. It was written about Asbury Park but took on a different tone in the wake of the September 11 attacks. That tone continued on *The Rising*, his 2002 album with the E Street Band, which weighed the consequences of the attacks and their aftermath. Beginning on the Rising tour, Springsteen became an adamant critic of the U.S. government, especially regarding the Iraq War. Springsteen's 2005 solo tour, following the release of the *Devils and Dust* album, explored the full depth of his song catalog and continued his opposition to the administration's policies.

We Shall Overcome: The Seeger Sessions (2006) took a turn unanticipated by even the closest Springsteen observers. He made the recording over a period of 10 years with a folk-roots band and a horn section. It featured traditional American folk songs ("Oh, Mary, Don't You Weep,"

"Froggie Went A-Courtin'," and "John Henry") as well as songs associated with its inspiration, Pete Seeger ("My Oklahoma Home," "How Can I Keep from Singing," and "Bring 'Em Home"). Springsteen's tour of the United States and Europe in 2006 featured a 20-piece band.

Magic (2007), another E Street Band album, spoke sometimes metaphorically and sometimes explicitly in opposition to the war and government intrusions on civil liberties. Springsteen continued his commentary through a worldwide tour with the E Street Band in 2007 and 2008. After the April 2008 death of the E Street Band organist and accordionist Danny Federici from melanoma, the band's playing acquired a darker urgency of tone. The later stages of the *Magic* tour featured arguably the most assertive, inspired playing Springsteen and the group had ever done.

Working on a Dream, released in early 2009, concerned itself lyrically with thoughts of love and life, how fleeting both are and what it takes to stay the course. The music on the album was a much more sophisticated version of what Springsteen had done on his first two albums, with a greater emphasis on harmony, especially vocal harmonies characteristic of the later work of the Beach Boys. In the lyrics, Springsteen's knack for particular detail served him well.

On Feb. 1, 2009, Springsteen and the band were the featured entertainment at halftime of Super Bowl XLIII; with an average viewership of 98.7 million, the game was the most-watched televised sports event in American history. Many fans and much of the press criticized Springsteen for commercializing himself this way. But in the aftermath, it was generally agreed that he had managed to condense the structure, message, humor, and athleticism of his live show into the 12 minutes allotted. On the largest popular culture platform available, Springsteen established that some rock artists remained determined to sustain their vitality and creative ambitions all the way to the end.

STEVIE WONDER

(b. May 13, 1950, Saginaw, Mich., U.S.)

American singer, songwriter, and multi-instrumentalist, Stevie Wonder was a child prodigy who developed into one of the most creative musical figures of the late 20th century.

Blind from birth and raised in inner-city Detroit, he was a skilled musician by age eight. Renamed Little Stevie Wonder by Berry Gordy, Jr., the president of Motown Records—to whom he was introduced by Ronnie White, a member of the Miracles—Wonder made his recording debut at age 12. The soulful quality of his high-pitched singing and the frantic harmonica playing that characterized his early recordings were evident in his first hit single, "Fingertips (Part 2)," recorded during a show at Chicago's Regal Theatre in 1963. But Wonder was much more than a freakish prepubescent imitation of Ray Charles, as audiences discovered when he demonstrated his prowess with piano, organ, harmonica, and drums. By 1964 he was no longer described as "Little," and two years later his fervent delivery of the pounding soul of "Uptight (Everything's Alright)," which he also had written, suggested the emergence of both an unusually compelling performer and a composer to rival Motown's stable of skilled songwriters. (He had already cowritten, with Smokey Robinson, "The Tears of a Clown.")

Over the next five years Wonder had hits with "I Was Made to Love Her," "My Cherie Amour" (both cowritten with producer Henry Cosby), and "For Once in My Life," songs that suited dancers as well as lovers. *Where I'm Coming From*, an album released in 1971, hinted not merely at an expanded musical range but, in its lyrics and its mood, at a new introspection. *Music of My Mind* (1972) made his concerns even more plain. In the interim he had been strongly influenced by Marvin Gaye's *What's Going On*, the album in which his Motown stablemate moved away from the label's "hit factory" approach to confront the divisive social issues of the day. Any anxieties Gordy may have felt about his protégé's declaration of independence were amply calmed by the run of recordings with which Wonder obliterated the competition in the mid-1970s. Those albums produced a steady stream of classic hit songs, among them "Superstition," "You Are the Sunshine of My Life," "Higher Ground," "Living for the City," "Don't You Worry 'Bout a Thing," "Boogie on Reggae Woman," "I Wish," and "Sir Duke."

Although still only in his mid-20s, Wonder appeared to have mastered virtually every idiom of African-American popular music and to have synthesized them all into a language of his own. His command of the new generation of electronic keyboard instruments made him a pioneer and an inspiration to rock musicians, the inventiveness of his vocal phrasing was reminiscent of the greatest jazz singers, and the depth and honesty of his emotional projection came straight from the Black church music of his childhood. Such a fertile period was unlikely to last forever, and it came to an end in 1979 with a fey and overambitious extended work called *Stevie Wonder's Journey Through the Secret Life of Plants*. Thereafter his recordings became sporadic and often lacked focus, although his concerts were never less than rousing. The best of his work formed a vital link between the classic rhythm-and-blues and soul performers of the 1950s and '60s and their less commercially constrained successors. Yet, however sophisticated his music became, he was never too proud to write something as apparently slight as the romantic gem "I Just Called to Say I Love You" (1984). He was inducted into the Rock and Roll Hall of Fame in 1989 and received a Grammy Award for lifetime achievement in 2005. In 2008 the Library of Congress announced that Wonder was the recipient of its Gershwin Prize for Popular Song.

THE SEX PISTOLS

The original members were Johnny Rotten (byname of John Lydon; b. Jan. 31, 1956, London, Eng.), Steve Jones (b. May 3, 1955, London, Eng.), Paul Cook (b. July 20, 1956, London, Eng.), and Glen Matlock (b. Aug. 27, 1956, London, Eng.). A later member was Sid Vicious (byname of John Simon Ritchie; b. May 10, 1957, London, Eng.—d. Feb. 2, 1979, New York, N.Y., U.S.).

The Sex Pistols created the British punk movement of the late 1970s and, with the song "God Save the Queen," became a symbol of the United Kingdom's social and political turmoil.

Thrown together in September 1975 by manager Malcolm McLaren to promote Sex, his London clothing store, the Sex Pistols began mixing 1960s English pop music influences (the Small Faces, the Who) with those of 1970s rock renegades (Iggy and the Stooges, the New York Dolls) in an attempt to strip rock's complexities to the bone. By the summer of 1976 the Sex Pistols had attracted an avid fan base and successfully updated the energies of the 1960s mods for the malignant teenage mood of the '70s. Heavily stylized in their image and music, media-savvy, and ambitious in their use of lyrics, the Sex Pistols became the leaders of a new teenage movement—called punk by the British press—in the autumn of 1976. Their first single, "Anarchy in the U.K.," was both a call to arms and a state-of-the-nation address. When they used profanity on live television in December 1976, the group became a national sensation. Scandalized in the tabloid press, the Sex Pistols were dropped by their first record company, EMI, in January 1977; their next contract, with A&M Records, was severed after only a few days in March.

Signing quickly with Virgin Records, the Sex Pistols released their second single, "God Save the Queen," in June 1977 to coincide with Queen Elizabeth II's Silver Jubilee (the 25th anniversary of her accession to the throne). Although banned by the British media, the single rose rapidly to number two on the charts. As "public enemies number one," the Sex Pistols were subjected to physical violence and harassment.

Despite a second Top Ten record, "Pretty Vacant," the Sex Pistols stalled. Barely able to play in the United Kingdom because of local government bans, they became mired in preparations for a film and the worsening drug use of Rotten's friend Vicious, who had replaced Matlock in February 1977. Their bunker mentality is evident on their third Top Ten hit, "Holidays in the Sun." By the time their album *Never Mind the Bollocks, Here's the Sex Pistols* reached number one in early November, Rotten, Vicious, Jones, and Cook had recorded together for the last time.

A short, disastrous U.S. tour precipitated the group's split in January 1978 following their biggest show to date, in San Francisco. Attempting to keep the Sex Pistols going with the film project that became *The Great Rock 'n' Roll Swindle* (1980), McLaren issued records with an increasingly uncontrollable Vicious as the vocalist. A cover version of Eddie Cochran's "C'mon Everybody" became the group's best-selling single following Vicious's fatal heroin overdose in New York City in February 1979 while out on bail (charged with the murder of his girlfriend, Nancy Spungen). That same month McLaren was sued by Rotten, and the Sex Pistols disappeared into receivership, only to be revived some years after the 1986 court case that restored control of their affairs to the group. A reunion tour in 1996 finally allowed the original quartet to play their hit songs in front of supportive audiences. This anticlimactic postscript, however, did not lessen the impact of their first four singles and debut album, which shook the foundations of rock music and sent tremors through British society. In 2006 the Sex Pistols were inducted into the Rock and Roll Hall of Fame.

PRINCE

(b. June 7, 1958, Minneapolis, Minn., U.S.—d. April 21, 2016, Chanhassen, Minn.)

Prince (born Prince Rogers Nelson) was a singer, guitarist, songwriter, producer, dancer, and performer on keyboards, drums, and bass who was among the most talented American musicians of his generation. A considerable number of his recordings feature him in all the performing roles.

Prince's recording career began with funk and soul marketed to a Black audience; his early music also reflected the contemporary musical impact of disco. Later records incorporated a vast array of influences, including jazz, punk, heavy metal, the Beatles, and hip-hop, usually within an overall approach most informed by funky up-tempo styles and soulful ballads; the latter often featured his expressive falsetto singing.

Taking an early interest in music, Prince began playing the piano at age 7 and mastered the guitar and drums by the time he joined his first band at age 14. With very few African American residents, his hometown, Minneapolis, Minnesota, was an unlikely site for the development of a major Black star, but Prince even managed to lead other local musicians, most notably Jimmy Jam and Terry Lewis, to major success.

Mirrored by correspondingly intense music, Prince's lyrics often address sexuality and desire with frankness and imagination. Much of his work, in its lyrics and imagery, struggles with the constriction of social conventions and categories. As one of his biographers put it, "The whole thrust of Prince's art can be understood in terms of a desire to escape the social identities thrust upon him by simple virtue of his being small, Black, and male."

Prince explored typographical oddities in his song titles and lyrics as another way of evading convention. In 1993 he announced that he had changed his name to a combination of the male and female gender signs. There is also a strong religious impulse in some of his music, sometimes fused into a kind of sacred erotic experience that has roots in African American churches.

"Little Red Corvette" (1983) was Prince's first big crossover hit, gaining airplay on MTV at a time when virtually no Black artists appeared on the influential new medium. *Purple Rain* (1984) made him one of the major stars of the 1980s and remains his biggest-selling album. Three of its singles were hits: the frenetic "Let's Go Crazy," the androgynous but vulnerable "When Doves Cry," and the anthemic title cut. Thereafter he continued to produce inventive music of broad appeal; outside the United States he was particularly popular in Britain and the rest of Europe.

Throughout most of his career, Prince's prolific inventiveness as a songwriter clashed with his record company's policy of releasing only a single album each year. As a backlog of his completed but unreleased recordings piled up, he gave songs to other performers—some of whom recorded at and for Paisley Park, the studio and label he established in suburban Minneapolis—and even organized ostensibly independent groups, such as the Time, to record his material. His 1996 album *Emancipation* celebrated the forthcoming

Prince performs in Brussels, Belgium, in 1986,

end of his Warner Brothers contract, which enabled him to release as much music as he liked on his NPG label. Later he explored marketing his work on the Internet and through private arrangements with retail chains as a means of circumventing the control of large record companies. In 1999, however, he released *Rave Un2 the Joy Fantastic* under the Arista label; a collaboration with Sheryl Crow, Chuck D, Ani DiFranco, and others, the album received mixed reviews and failed to find a large audience. Prince (who, following the formal termination of his contract with Warner Brothers in 1999, stopped using the symbol as his name) was inducted into the Rock and Roll Hall of Fame in 2004. That year he also released *Musicology*, an album that both sold well and was much praised by critics.

MADONNA

(b. Aug. 16, 1958, Bay City, Mich., U.S.)

The immense popularity in the 1980s and '90s of American singer, songwriter, actress, and entrepreneur Madonna (born Madonna Louise Ciccone) allowed her to achieve levels of power and control unprecedented for a woman in the entertainment industry.

Born into a large Italian-American family, Madonna studied dance at the University of Michigan and with the Alvin Ailey American Dance Theater in New York City in the late 1970s before relocating briefly to Paris as a member of Patrick Hernandez's disco revue. Returning to New York City, she performed with a number of rock groups before signing with Sire Records. Her first hit, "Holiday," in 1983, provided the blueprint for her later material—an upbeat dance-club sound with sharp production and an immediate appeal. Madonna's melodic pop incorporated catchy choruses and her lyrics concerned love, sex, and relationships—ranging from the breezy innocence of "True Blue" (1986) to the erotic fantasies of "Justify My Love" (1990) to the spirituality of later songs such as "Ray of Light" (1998). Criticized by some as being limited in range, her sweet, girlish voice nonetheless was well-suited to pop music.

Madonna was the first female artist to exploit fully the potential of the music video. She collaborated with top designers (Jean-Paul Gaultier), photographers (Steven Meisel and Herb Ritts), and directors (Mary Lambert and David Fincher), drawing inspiration from underground club culture or the avant-garde to create distinctive sexual and satirical images—from the knowing ingenue of "Like a Virgin" (1984) to the controversial red-dressed "sinner" who kisses a Black saint in "Like a Prayer" (1989). By 1991 she had scored 21 Top Ten hits in the United States and sold some 70 million albums internationally, generating $1.2 billion in sales. Committed to controlling her image and career herself, Madonna became the head of Maverick, a subsidiary of Time-Warner created by the entertainment giant as part of a $60 million deal with the performer. Her success signaled a clear message of financial control to other women in the industry, but in terms of image she was a more ambivalent role model.

In 1992 Madonna took her role as a sexual siren to its full extent when she published *Sex*, a soft-core pornographic coffee-table book featuring her in a variety of "erotic" poses. She was criticized for being exploitative and overcalculating, and writer Norman Mailer said she had become "secretary to herself." Soon afterward Madonna temporarily withdrew from pop music to concentrate on a film career that had begun with a strong performance in *Desperately Seeking Susan* (1985), faltered with the flimsy *Shanghai Surprise* (1986) and *Dick Tracy* (1990), and recovered with *Truth or Dare* (1991, also known as *In Bed with Madonna*), a documentary of one of her tours. She scored massive success in 1996 with the starring role in the film musical *Evita*. That year she also gave birth to a daughter.

In 1998 Madonna released her first album of new material in four years, *Ray of Light*. A fusion of techno music and self-conscious lyrics, it was a commercial and critical success, earning the singer her first musical Grammy Awards (her previous win had been for a video). Her experimentation in electronica continued with *Music* (2000). In 2005 she returned to her roots with *Confessions on a Dance Floor*. Despite a marriage in the 1980s to actor Sean Penn and another to English director Guy Ritchie (married 2000; divorced 2008), with whom she had two sons, Madonna remained resolutely independent. That independent streak, however, did not prevent her from enlisting the biggest names in music to assist on specific projects. This fact was clear on *Hard Candy* (2008), a hip-hop infused effort with writing and vocal and production work by Justin Timberlake, Timbaland, and Pharrell Williams of the hit-making duo The Neptunes. In 2008 she was inducted into the Rock and Roll Hall of Fame.

MICHAEL JACKSON

(b. Aug. 29, 1958, Gary, Ind., U.S.—d. June 25, 2009, Los Angeles, Calif., U.S.)

American singer, songwriter, and dancer Michael Joseph Jackson was the most popular entertainer in the world in the early and mid-1980s. Reared in Gary, Ind., in one of the most acclaimed musical families of the rock era, Michael Jackson was the youngest and most talented of five brothers whom his father, Joseph, shaped into a dazzling group of child stars known as the Jackson 5. In addition to Michael, the members of the Jackson 5 (all also born in Gary) were Jackie Jackson (b. May 4, 1951), Tito Jackson (b. Oct. 15, 1953), Jermaine Jackson (b. Dec. 11, 1954), and Marlon Jackson (b. March 12, 1957).

Motown Records president Berry Gordy, Jr., was impressed with the group and signed them in 1969. Sporting the loudest fashions, the largest Afros, the snappiest choreography, and a youthful, soulful exuberance, the Jackson 5 became an immediate success. They scored four consecutive number one pop hits with "I Want You Back," "ABC," "The Love You Save," and "I'll Be There" in 1970. With Michael topping the pop charts as a solo performer with "Ben" and reaching number two with "Rockin' Robin," and with the Jackson 5 producing trendsetting dance tracks such as *Dancing Machine*, the family's string of hits for Motown lasted through 1975. As Michael matured, his voice changed, family tensions arose, and a contract standoff ensued. The group finally broke with Motown, moving to Epic Records as the Jacksons. Jermaine remained at Motown as a solo performer and was replaced by his youngest brother, Randy Jackson (b. Oct. 29, 1961). As a recording act, the Jacksons enjoyed consistent success through 1984, and their sister Janet Jackson embarked on her own singing career in the early 1980s; however, Michael's solo albums took on an entirely different status.

Jackson's first solo effort for Epic, *Off the Wall* (1979), exceeded all expectations and was the best-selling album of the year. Produced by industry veteran Quincy Jones, *Off the Wall* yielded the massive international hit singles "Don't Stop 'til You Get Enough" and "Rock with You," both of which showcased Michael's energetic style and capitalized on the contemporary disco dance fad. Three years later he returned with another collaboration with

Jones, *Thriller*, a tour de force that featured an array of guest stars and elevated him to a worldwide superstar. *Thriller* sold more than 40 million copies, captured a slew of awards, including a record-setting eight Grammys, and became the best-selling album in history. The first single on the album, "The Girl Is Mine," an easygoing duet with Paul McCartney, went to number one on the rhythm-and-blues charts and number two on the pop charts in the fall of 1982. The follow-up single, "Billie Jean," an electrifying dance track and the vehicle for Jackson's trademark "moonwalk" dance, topped the pop charts, as did "Beat It," which featured a raucous solo from famed guitarist Eddie Van Halen. Moreover, "Beat It" helped break down the artificial barriers between Black and white artists on the radio and in the emerging format of music videos on television.

By 1984 Jackson was renowned worldwide as the "King of Pop." His much anticipated Victory reunion tour with his brothers was one of the most popular concert events of 1984. Further solo albums—*Bad* (1987) and *Dangerous* (1991)—solidified Jackson's dominance of pop music, and in 2001 he was inducted into the Rock and Roll Hall of Fame; the Jackson 5 were inducted in 1997.

Jackson's eccentric, secluded lifestyle grew increasingly controversial in the early 1990s. His reputation was seriously damaged in 1993 when he was accused of child molestation by a 13-year-old boy he had befriended; a civil suit was settled out of court. In 1994 Jackson secretly married Lisa Marie Presley, daughter of Elvis Presley, but their marriage lasted less than two years. Shortly thereafter Jackson married again, this marriage producing children, though it, too, ended in divorce. While he remained an international celebrity, his image in the United States was slow to recover, and it suffered even more in November 2003 when he was arrested and charged with child molestation. After a 14-week trial that became something of a media

Michael Jackson's Dangerous World Tour took place in 1993.

circus, Jackson was acquitted in 2005.

The singer was preparing a comeback tour in 2009 when he died suddenly of cardiac arrest. A widespread outpouring of grief culminated in a memorial celebration of his life on July 7, 2009 at the Staples Center in Los Angeles.

PUBLIC ENEMY

The original members were Chuck D (original name Carlton Ridenhour; b. Aug. 1, 1960, New York, N.Y., U.S.), Flavor Flav (original name William Drayton; b. March 16, 1959, New York, N.Y., U.S.), Terminator X (original name Norman Lee Rogers; b. Aug. 25, 1966, New York, N.Y., U.S.), and Professor Griff (original name Richard Griffin).

Public Enemy was an American rap group whose dense, layered sound and radical political message made them among the most popular, controversial, and influential hip-hop artists of the late 1980s and early '90s.

Public Enemy was formed in 1982 at Adelphi University on Long Island, New York, by a group of African Americans who came primarily from the suburbs. Chuck D, Hank Shocklee, Bill Stephney, and Flavor Flav collaborated on a program on college radio. Reputedly, Def Jam producer Rick Rubin was so taken with Chuck D's booming voice that he begged him to record. Public Enemy resulted and brought radical Black political ideology to pop music in an unprecedented fashion on albums with titles that read like party invitations for leftists and warning stickers for the right wing: *Yo! Bum Rush the Show* (1987), *It Takes a Nation of Millions to Hold Us Back* (1988), *Fear of a Black Planet* (1990), and *Apocalypse 91: The Enemy Strikes Black* (1991).

Acclaimed as Public Enemy's masterpiece, *Nation of Millions* revived the messages of the Black Panther Party and Malcolm X. On tracks such as "Night of the Living Baseheads," "Black Steel in the Hour of Chaos," and "Don't Believe the Hype," the strident, eloquent lyrics of

Chuck D combined with bombastic, dissonant, and poignantly detailed backing tracks created by Public Enemy's production team, the Bomb Squad (Shocklee, his brother Keith, Chuck D, and Eric "Vietnam" Adler), to produce songs challenging the status quo in both hip-hop and racial politics. The Bomb Squad sampled (composed with other recordings) a wide variety of genres and sounds, including classic funk tracks by James Brown, jazz, the thrash-metal of Anthrax, sirens, and agitprop speeches. Flavor Flav provided a comic foil for Chuck D.

Comments by Professor Griff to the *Washington Times* in 1989 brought charges of anti-Semitism, which ultimately resulted in his leaving the group. Public Enemy's open admiration for the Nation of Islam leader Louis Farrakhan also brought it into conflict with Jewish organizations. While Public Enemy's activism inspired other artists to take up topical themes, the group's influence waned in the early 1990s as younger, more "ghetto-centric" performers such as N.W.A. and Snoop Doggy Dogg came to the fore. The group seemed to have folded after *Muse Sick N Hour Mess Age* (1994), but in 1998 they produced a new album of songs for Spike Lee's film *He Got Game* and went on tour.

U2

The members are Bono (byname of Paul Hewson; b. May 10, 1960, Dublin, Ire.), the Edge (byname of David Evans; b. Aug. 8, 1961, Barking, Essex [now in Greater London], Eng.), Adam Clayton (b. March 13, 1960, Oxford, Oxfordshire, Eng.), and Larry Mullen, Jr. (b. Oct. 31, 1961, Dublin, Ire.).

Irish postpunk band U2 had established itself by the end of the 1980s not only as one of the world's most popular bands but also as one of the most innovative.

Though forged in the crucible of punk rock that swept Europe in the late 1970s, U2 instantly created a distinctive identity with its grandiose sound; a merger of the Edge's minimal, reverb-drenched guitar; and Bono's quasi-operatic vocals. The band members were attending a Dublin secondary school when they began rehearsing, undeterred by their lack of technical expertise. The band's early records were characterized by an intense spirituality, and they commented on social and political issues, such as the civil strife in Northern Ireland, with compassion and tenderness. The group became renowned for its inspirational live performances and was a word-of-mouth sensation long before it made much of an impact on the pop charts. But, with the multimillion-selling success of *The Joshua Tree* album (1987) and the number one hits "With or Without You" and "I Still Haven't Found What I'm Looking For," U2 became pop stars. On *Rattle and Hum* (1988), a double album and documentary movie, the band explored American roots music—blues, country, gospel, and folk—with typical earnestness but were pilloried by some critics who found the project pompous.

U2 reinvented itself for the new decade, reemerging in 1991 with the album *Achtung Baby* and a sound heavily influenced by European experimental, electronic, and disco music. With this came a stage show that trafficked in irony and self-deprecating humour, qualities virtually absent from the band's music in the previous decade; the 1992 Zoo TV tour was one of the most technically ambitious and artistically accomplished large-scale rock spectacles ever staged. But, despite the flashier exterior, the band's lyrics remained obsessed with matters of the soul. The dehumanizing aspects of media and technology were a recurring theme on subsequent records, even as the band immersed itself in techno textures.

In 1997 the band rush-released the *Pop* album to fulfill

obligations for a stadium tour and was greeted with its worst reviews since *Rattle and Hum*. Another reinvention was in store, but this time, rather than boldly pushing forward, the band sought to reassure fans by making music that referenced its 1980s roots. The aptly titled *All That You Can't Leave Behind* (2000) and *How to Dismantle an Atomic Bomb* (2004) were focused on riffs and songs rather than atmosphere and mystery, and they succeeded in reestablishing the quartet as a commercial force, but at what price? The band took five years before releasing its 12th studio album, *No Line on the Horizon* (2009). Longtime collaborators Brian Eno and Daniel Lanois played a bigger role in the production and songwriting, and the layered textures of the album's most experimental work crept back prominently in the mix.

NIRVANA

The members were Kurt Cobain (b. Feb. 20, 1967, Aberdeen, Wash., U.S.—d. April 5, 1994, Seattle, Wash.), Krist Novoselic (b. May 16, 1965, Compton, Calif., U.S.), and Dave Grohl (b. Jan. 14, 1969, Warren, Ohio, U.S.).

Nirvana was an American alternative rock group whose breakthrough album, *Nevermind* (1991), announced a new musical style (grunge) and gave voice to the post-baby boom young adults known as Generation X.

From Aberdeen, near Seattle, Nirvana was part of the postpunk underground scene that centred on K Records of Olympia, Washington, before they recorded their first single, "Love Buzz," and album, *Bleach*, for Sub Pop, an independent record company in Seattle. They refined this mix of 1960s-style pop and 1970s heavy metal–hard rock on their first album for a major label, Geffen; *Nevermind*, featuring the anthemic hit "Smells Like Teen Spirit," was the first full expression of punk concerns to

Kurt Cobain of Nirvana performs in Slovenia in 1994, months before his death.

achieve mass market success in the United States.

Nirvana used extreme changes of tempo and volume to express anger and alienation: a quiet, tuneful verse switched into a ferocious, distorted chorus. In the fashion of many 1970s punk groups, guitarist-singer-songwriter Cobain set powerful rock against sarcastic, allusive lyrics that explored hopelessness, surrender, and male abjection ("As a defense I'm neutered and spayed," he sang in "On a Plain"). Imbued with the punk ethic that to succeed was to fail, Nirvana abhorred the media onslaught that accompanied their rapid ascent. Success brought celebrity, and Cobain, typecast as a self-destructive rock star, courted controversy both with his advocacy of feminism and gay rights and with his embroilment in a sequence of drug- and gun-related escapades—a number of which involved his wife, Courtney Love, leader of the band Hole.

Like *Nevermind*, the band's third album, *In Utero* (1993)—which contained clear articulations of Cobain's psyche in songs such as "All Apologies" and "Rape Me"—reached number one on the U.S. album charts. By this point, however, Cobain's heroin use was out of control. After a reputed suicide attempt in Rome in March 1994, he entered a Los Angeles treatment center. In a mysterious sequence of events, he returned to Seattle, where he shot and killed himself in his lakeside home. Subsequent concert releases, notably *Unplugged in New York* (1994) and *From the Muddy Banks of the Wishkah* (1996), only added to Nirvana's legend. In 2002 the greatest-hits album *Nirvana* appeared and included the previously unreleased single "You Know You're Right." That year a collection of Cobain's journals was also published.

RADIOHEAD

Formed in the mid-1980s at Abingdon School in Oxfordshire, Radiohead comprised singer-guitarist Thom Yorke (b. Oct. 7, 1968, Wellingborough, Northamptonshire, Eng.), bassist Colin Greenwood (b. June 26, 1969, Oxford, Oxfordshire, Eng.), guitarist Ed O'Brien (b. April 15, 1968, Oxford, Oxfordshire, Eng.), drummer Phil Selway (b. May 23, 1967, Hemingford Grey, Huntingdon, Cambridgeshire, Eng.), and guitarist-keyboardist Jonny Greenwood (b. Nov. 5, 1971, Oxford, Oxfordshire, Eng.).

The British rock group Radiohead arguably has been the most accomplished art-rock band of the early 21st century. This revered quintet made some of the most majestic—if most angst-saturated—music of the post-modern era.

Strongly influenced by American bands such as R.E.M. and the Pixies, Radiohead paid early dues on the local pub circuit. With their university education completed, the group landed a deal with Parlophone in late 1991. Although its debut album, *Pablo Honey* (1993), barely hinted at the grandeur to come, the startling single "Creep"—a grungy snarl of self-loathing—made major waves in the United States.

The Bends (1995) took even the band's most ardent fans by surprise. A soaring, intense mix of the approaches of Nirvana and dramatic vocalist Jeff Buckley, the album's powerful sense of alienation completely transcended the parochial issues of mid-1990s Britpop. Driving rockers such as "Bones" were skillfully offset by sad ballads such as "High and Dry." The widely acclaimed *OK Computer* (1997) was nothing short of a premillennial version of Pink Floyd's classic album *Dark Side of the Moon* (1973): huge-sounding and chillingly beautiful, with Yorke's weightless voice enveloped on masterpieces such as "Lucky" by webs of dark, dense textures. In its live performances, Radiohead became one of pop music's most compelling acts.

The pressure to follow up one of the most acclaimed recordings of the 20th century told particularly on Yorke's fragile psyche. The band made false starts in Paris and Copenhagen before settling down back in England. When *Kid A* came out in October 2000, it signaled that Radiohead—and Yorke above all—wanted to leave the wide-screen drama of *OK Computer* behind. The resulting selection of heavily electronic, more or less guitar-free pieces (notably "Kid A" and "Idioteque") confounded many but repaid the patience of fans who stuck with it. Though the album was a commercial success, it met with mixed critical reaction, as would the similar *Amnesiac* (2001), produced during the same sessions as *Kid A*. But if Radiohead had seemingly disavowed its musical past on these two albums—moving away from melody and rock instrumentation to create intricately textured soundscapes—it found a way to meld this approach with its guitar-band roots on the much-anticipated album *Hail to the Thief* (2003), which reached number three on the U.S. album charts. In 2006 Yorke, who had reluctantly become for some the voice of his generation, collaborated with the group's modernist producer, Nigel Godrich, on a solo album, *The Eraser*.

The band, having concluded its six-album contract with the EMI Group in 2003, broke away from major label distribution and initially released its seventh album, *In Rainbows* (2007), via Internet download. An estimated 1.2 million fans downloaded the album within its first week of availability, paying any price they wished to do so. The novel distribution method generated headlines, but it was the album's content—a collection of 10 tracks that served as a confident, almost optimistic, sonic counterpoint to *The Bends*—that led critics to declare it the most approachable Radiohead album in a decade.

In Rainbows was released to retailers as a standard CD in 2008, and it immediately hit number one in both the United States and Great Britain. The group won its third Grammy for the album, and the *In Rainbows* box set, which featured CD and vinyl copies of the original tracks, a CD of eight bonus songs, and a booklet of original artwork, received the Grammy for limited edition packaging.

JAY-Z

(b. Dec. 4, 1970, Brooklyn, N.Y., U.S.)

American rapper and entrepreneur Jay-Z (born Shawn Corey Carter) was one of the most influential figures in hip-hop in the 1990s and 2000s.

Shawn Carter grew up in Brooklyn's often dangerous Marcy Projects, where he was raised mainly by his mother. His firsthand experience with illicit drug dealing would inform his lyrics when he began rapping under the stage name Jazzy, soon shortened to Jay-Z (a name that may also have been derived from the proximity of the J and Z subway lines to the Marcy Projects). Jay-Z and two friends founded their own company, Roc-a-Fella Records, to release his debut album, *Reasonable Doubt* (1996), which climbed the *Billboard* charts, reaching number 23 on the pop chart and number 3 on the rhythm-and-blues chart.

A string of successful albums followed at a rate of at least one per year through 2003. *Vol. 2: Hard Knock Life* (1998) not only was the first of Jay-Z's releases to top the *Billboard* 200 album sales chart but also won a Grammy Award for best rap album. In 2001 he pleaded guilty to assault relating to a 1999 nightclub stabbing and received three years' probation. In 2003, with the release of *The Black Album*, Jay-Z announced his retirement as a performer. In 2004 he assumed the presidency of Def Jam Recordings, making him one of the most highly placed African American executives in the recording industry at the time.

Postretirement, Jay-Z stayed remarkably active, collaborating with the rock group Linkin Park in 2004 and appearing as a guest vocalist on the recordings of numerous other artists, including Kanye West and Beyoncé; Jay-Z and Beyoncé were married in 2008. He developed a large portfolio of business ventures and investments, including Roc-a-Fella Films, a clothing line, and a stake in the New Jersey Nets of the National Basketball Association. He formally returned to recording in 2006 with *Kingdom Come*. In December 2007 he stepped down as Def Jam president shortly after releasing the album *American Gangster*. Jay-Z proved that he remained one of rap's most bankable acts when he embarked on a highly successful tour with Mary J. Blige in 2008. The following year he won a Grammy Award for best rap performance for *Swagga Like Us*, a collaboration with T.I., Kanye West, and Lil Wayne.

Glossary

agitprop: Political propaganda in the form of art, music, literature, film, etc.

amalgam: A fusion of different elements.

androgynous: Having both male and female characteristics.

avant-garde: Experimental or progressive.

Britpop: Popular music from Britain in the 1990s, often brighter and more melodic than alternative or grunge rock that was also popular during the time period.

diurnal: Active during the day, as opposed to during the night (nocturnal).

eponymous: Named after a particular person; self-titled.

pastiche: A musical or other artistic style that mimics a previous style or artwork.

prolix: Using an excess of words or long and drawn out.

vibrato: A rapid, repetitive fluctuation of pitch on a sustained vocal or instrumental tone.

virtuoso: An exceptionally skilled musician or artist.

Yoruba: A language used in Nigeria and parts of Benin and Togo, or a person who speaks the language in these regions.

zeitgeist: The general culture of a period.

For More Information

BOOKS

Marley, Ziggy. *Bob Marley: Portrait of the Legend.* New York, NY: Rizzoli, 2020.

Norman, Philip. *Wild Thing: The Short, Spellbinding Life of Jimi Hendrix.* New York, NY: Liveright Publishing Corporation, 2020.

O'Neill, Terry. *David Bowie.* London, England: Cassell Illustrated, 2019.

Spiotta, Dana. *Kurt Cobain: The Last Interview and Other Conversations.* Brooklyn, NY: Melville House, 2022.

WEBSITES

Classic Motown

www.classic.motown.com

Learn more about the history of Motown Records, which gave its name to an entire subgenre of rhythm and blues music in the 1960s and 1970s.

The 50th Anniversary of Hip-Hop

www.the50thanniversaryofhip-hop.com

Celebrate half a century of hip-hop by visiting this website from Legends Recordings.

Rock & Roll Hall of Fame

www.rockhall.com

Read more about artists that have been inducted to the Rock & Roll Hall of Fame and find out how to visit the museum.

Index